Cognitive Behavioral

Therapy

How to Free Yourself from Your

Inner Monologue and Eliminate

Negative Self Forever

By

Stuart Killan

Stuart Killan

entertainment purposes only. All effort has been executed to present accurate, up to date, and reliable, complete information. No warranties of any kind are declared or implied. Readers acknowledge that the author is not engaging in the rendering of legal, financial, medical or professional advice. The content within this book has been derived from various sources. Please consult a licensed professional before attempting any techniques outlined in this book.

By reading this document, the reader agrees that under no circumstances is the author responsible for any losses, direct or indirect, which are incurred as a result of the use of information contained within this document, including, but not limited to, — errors, omissions, or inaccuracies.

Stuart Killan

Table Of Contents

Your Free Gift

As a way of saying thank you for downloading. I'm offering a free bonus report called ***7 Habits of Highly Confident People*** that's exclusive to the readers of this book.

Get instant access at http://freeconfidencebook.com

Inside the book you'll discover

- Secrets of The Joker, and why he should be admired
- The one thing confident people *always* do first when confronted with a tough situation – learning this alone can 10X your self esteem
- How to use vision boards to achieve your goals
- Identifying your "hidden talents" – even if you don't think you have any

Stuart Killan

- The one trait you must MURDER if you are to become successful
- How to never doubt your own abilities again
- Michael Jordan's #1 success secret
- The 4 most dangerous words in your vocabulary (if you're saying these regularly you are killing your own confidence)
- How to succeed as an introvert in an extrovert's world

Download for free at http://freeconfidencebook.com

Introduction

I want to thank you for purchasing the book, 'Shyness: How to Free Yourself from Your Inner Monologue and Eliminate Negative Self-Talk Forever.'

Everybody, including the most successful people, often have a voice in the back of their head telling them that they are not good enough. We do not talk about it since we are afraid that people will think of us as weak individuals. It is easy for people to tell you to live in the present and not overthink. But, what do they really mean by that?

The only way one can achieve happiness is by altering how they perceive themselves. You can never believe someone when they tell you that they are perfect since everybody has flaws. All you can do is believe in yourself and tell the voice inside your head to shut up. This book will help you learn how to shut the inner voice and believe in yourself.

Stuart Killan

Thank you once again for purchasing the book. I hope it helps you.

Chapter One: Negative Self-Talk and How it Affects You

Everybody has an inner critic that helps to motivate to achieve his or her goals. This critic helps you stick to a diet or lifestyle depending on what your goal is. However, if you do not check this voice, it will harm you, particularly if you are negative about life. This voice is called negative self-talk and it can bring you down before you realize what has happened to you.

Most people experience negative self-talk at least once in their lives, and this talk comes in multiple forms. You can also be under stress because of this talk thereby affecting the people around you if you are not careful. This chapter provides information on what negative self-talk is and how it affects your mind, body, life and your relationships.

What is Negative Self-Talk

Negative self-talk takes a variety of forms. For instance, it can help you stay grounded by telling you that there are somethings you must avoid to stay safe and healthy. There are times when it can sound mean by telling you that you can never do anything right. You can also use this voice to take a realistic approach or develop fear or a fantasy.

The musings or thoughts of your inner critic can sound like a critical friend or partner from the past. This voice can take the path of cognitive distortions like blaming and catastrophizing. In other words, negative self-talk is that voice inside you that limits your ability and prevents you from believing in yourself. These thoughts diminish your ability to change your life. Negative self-talk isn't just stressful, but it can also hinder your success.

How to Spot Negative Thinking

Let us look at some of the common forms of negative self-talk.

Filtering

Regardless of what the situation is, you will focus on the negative aspects of the situation and ignore the positive ones. For instance, let us say that you had a great day of work. You completed every task assigned to you on time and did a thorough job of it. People showered you with compliments. However, you forget about those compliments and only focus on the tasks that you were unable to complete. You then begin to work on more tasks and put yourself under stress.

Personalizing

When you are in a bad situation, you blame yourself regardless of whether you were at fault or not. For instance, if you hear that your friends cancelled on a night out, you will assume that nobody wanted to come because they did not want to be with you.

Catastrophizing

You always anticipate the worst in a situation. When you wake up and stub your toe, you tell yourself that you woke up on the wrong side of the bed. You convince yourself that you will have a horrible day.

Polarizing

Things or situations can only be good or bad. You never see the middle ground. Therefore, you strive to be perfect to ensure that every situation you are in is good. If there is ever a time when a situation is not in your favor, you convince yourself that you are a failure.

Toll of Negative Self-Talk

Negative self-talk has a disastrous effect on you. There are studies that link negative self-talk with low self-esteem and high levels of stress. This talk can lead to feelings of helplessness and demotivation. Therefore, it is important that you learn to fix this negative self-talk.

People who frequently engage in negative self-talk are often more stressed. This happens since their reality is slightly altered to help them experience the success they believe they have achieved. They need to create this experience since they do not see the many opportunities around them, and they do not capitalize on those opportunities. Therefore, the perception of stress is because of the change in behavior and perception. The consequences of the inner critic are listed below:

Limited Thinking

You constantly tell yourself that you cannot do something. The more you tell yourself that, you start to believe it. For example, if you tell yourself that you cannot pass an exam, you will start to believe it and eventually you will not pass that exam.

Perfectionism

You start to believe that you cannot just be great. You must be perfect and that you can attain that level of perfection. However, people who are high achievers often perform better than people who want to be perfectionists. This is because the former group of people are happier and less stressed when they do a job well. The latter often pick a task apart and see what they can do better next time.

Depressive Feelings and Emotions

Negative self-talk often leads to depressive feelings and emotions. This inner voice can lead to grave consequences if you do not check it early in life. For example, when you constantly tell yourself that you have no friends, you will start to feel depressed.

Challenges in Relationships

Negative self-talk changes the way you perceive yourself and others. It can turn you into an insecure and needy person. But, it makes you want to constantly criticize the people around you. It is because of this criticism that people will want to stay away from you.

An obvious drawback of negative self-talk is that it is not positive. It sounds simple, but research has shown that when you motivate yourself, you will succeed. For instance, a study was conducted on athletes where four types of self-talk were compared. It was found that positive self-talk helped an athlete succeed since they did not have to constantly remind themselves that they were doing great.

Chapter Two: How to Silence the Negative Talk

It is good to criticize yourself since it helps you become a better person. But, there is a great difference between telling yourself that you are a huge person and telling yourself that you should work out.

You should remember that your inner voice defines what success and failure is to you. When you criticize yourself excessively, it will backfire since you will focus more on failure. Instead of focusing on what you should have done better or what you should improve, you worry about the significance of the mistake. As mentioned earlier, negative self-talk is associated with depression and stress. This chapter gives you tips on how to stuff the muzzle of your inner critic.

Set Aside All the Negativity

When you beat yourself up, you inflate a small mistake into a huge failure. When you begin to think negatively, take a few deep breaths. Once you are calm, break the problem down into segments and identify a solution to the smaller problems. Try to change the way you perceive a mistake. For example, if you made a mistake during a meeting, instead of telling yourself that you screwed up, you can tell yourself that you made a mistake and should find a way to make up for that mistake. It helps if you can set aside the negative and visualize a positive environment. When you see that the problem fits into the smallest box possible, you will develop confidence.

Possible Thinking

People will always ask you to think positively when you are upset. However, research has found that saying positive things to yourself when you are upset only makes you feel worse.

This is because your brain defines these positive thoughts as lies. Experts suggest that you use a technique called possible thinking where you only reach for neutral thoughts about a situation. For example, "I am huge." becomes "I need to lose weight, and I know exactly how to do it." When you focus on the facts, you can choose which path you want to take.

Stop Questioning Yourself Self love

Let us assume that you were in a meeting and you blurted out that your bra was too tight. You tell yourself that you have made a fool of yourself. But, think about the situation – was everybody in the meeting paying attention to you or were they busy tapping on their phones?

One of the best ways to be kind to yourself is by questioning your thoughts. When you ask yourself more questions, you will feel better about some situations and not worry about what someone has to say about you. For example, instead of asking yourself, "How could I have been so stupid to say that in front of everybody?" tell yourself that you made a mistake and it is okay.

Change Your Outlook

Thinking Differently

Change the way you look at situations. Instead of telling yourself, "I cannot do this today. Serves me right for being disorganized." tell yourself, "I am not sure I can do this today."

This may seem silly, but a change in wording gives you the feeling that this moment is just a moment. When you tell yourself that you are stupid, you define who you are. However, when you say that you felt stupid, you convince yourself that you are not stupid, but only felt stupid in that moment.

Stuart Killan

Be Your Own Friend

When you make mistakes at work or in life, the first person you will share this mistake with is your friend. How does your friend react when you tell him or her something – "Are you sure it was that bad that it will ruin your career?"

Another thing to remember is that you should never tell yourself what you would not tell your friend. You know that you will never call your friend a slob if he or she drops food on his clothing. So, why should you call yourself one?

Name Your Critic Chunky McBrain Butt !!

Give your inner critic a silly name. It is difficult to take your critic seriously when you address it with a funny name. For example, Brene Brown, a professor at the University of Houston Graduate College of Social Work refers to her inner critic as the Gremlin! When you name the inner critic something funny, it will break the emotional hold that the voice has over you. This will in turn help you break the anxiety cycle.

Name Your Rants too

Some psychologists call these inner thoughts and rants stories. You can name every thought that passes through your mind and every memory you have ever made. When you take a step back and go through all the stories, you will realize that the premise to most stories is the same. The same thoughts pass through your mind regularly, which should help you understand that these are not thoughts but habits. These habits are not the truth.

Pick Up the Phone

You only feel shame when you keep everything a

secret. For example, if you went to a party and did something stupid, leave the place and call your friend. When you tell him or her what transpired at the party, he or she will laugh. At that moment, you will have cut off shame at the knees. Find the courage to speak to someone and laugh at yourself at what you did.

Embrace Your Flaws

It is important that you stop holding yourself to high standards. It is destructive to be a perfectionist. If you read an interview given by the CEO of a company, you will never hear them tell you that they are perfect. Instead, they credit their success to a mistake they made. They tell about what they learned from the mistake they made and how it shaped their goal.

Relax your standards a little and show yourself some empathy. You can win over the Nag with ease!

Cognitive Behavioral Therapy

Chapter Three: Positive Thinking

How do you answer this question – is your glass half-full or half-empty? I am sure you may have come across this question earlier. The answer to this question defines how you look at life and your attitude towards yourself. The answer to this question also affects your mental health.

Many studies have concluded that traits like pessimism and optimism affect many areas of your physical and mental wellbeing. When you are optimistic, you have a positive outlook on life. Therefore, you can manage your stress with ease thereby improving your mental wellbeing. If you are pessimistic and listen to your inner critic, do not fret. You can develop positive thinking skills.

Understand Positive Self-Talk and Positive Thinking

When someone says positive thinking, it does not necessarily mean that you should ignore the less pleasant situations in your life. When you think positively, you can approach an unpleasant situation in a productive and positive way. You begin to believe that the best will happen to you and not the worst.

Positive thinking starts with positive self-talk. You can transform all the stream of negative self-talk into positive talk using the tips mentioned in the previous chapter. Often, self-talk comes from reason and logic, but there are times when this talk arises from misconceptions that you create because you lack information.

Benefits of Positive Thinking

Experts continue to study the benefits of positive thinking on physical and mental health. Some benefits include:

- Lower levels of depression

- Increased life span

- Resistance to diseases like the common cold

- Lower levels of distress

- Better physical and psychological well-being

- Reduced risk of cardiovascular diseases

- Better heart health

- Better coping mechanisms during times of stress and hardship

Researchers must conduct further studies to understand how positive thinking benefits health. A theory is that when you think positively you can deal with stressful situations better. This reduces the effects that stress has on your body. People with a positive approach towards life lead healthier lifestyles since they follow a healthy diet, get more physical activity and do not drink or smoke in excess.

How to Focus on Positive Thinking

You can turn your negative thoughts into positive thoughts with ease. It is a simple process, but it takes practice and time. This is because you are developing a new habit. This section gives you some tips that you can use to start thinking positively.

Identify the Areas to Change

Before you begin to think positively, you should identify the areas in your life where you always think negatively. These areas can be work, relationships, your travel or education. You must start small and focus on one area. Try to approach any situation in that area positively before you move on to another area.

Check Yourself

Always stop and evaluate your thoughts at some

point during the day. If you find that you only have negative thoughts, identify a way to add some positivity to those thoughts.

Be Open to Humor

You must laugh or smile when you are in a difficult situation. Try to look for humor in every situation. If you can laugh when you are stressed, you will feel better and can take the world on with renewed energy.

Follow a Healthy Lifestyle

Exercise for at least 30 minutes every day on four or five days of the week. You can break the time up into ten-minute intervals and exercise any time during the day. Exercise is an activity that has a positive affect on your mood and helps to reduce stress. Follow a healthy diet to ensure that you have enough energy throughout the day.

Surround Yourself with Positive People

You must ensure that the people in your life are supportive, positive and you can depend on them when you are under stress. These people should be willing to give you advice when needed and give you constructive feedback when necessary. Negative people increase your stress levels and make you doubt your capabilities.

Practice Positive Self-Talk

As mentioned earlier, you should follow a simple rule – never tell yourself something you will not say to another person. Always be gentle with yourself and encourage yourself to do better. If you start to think negatively, evaluate the situation, and tell yourself what is good about you. Think about the things in your life that you are grateful for.

Stuart Killan

How to Practice Positive Thinking Every day

When you feel negativity in life, you cannot expect to turn into an optimist overnight. However, with practice your inner critic will become more of a friend. You will accept yourself for who you are and take your tasks up with renewed enthusiasm. When your state of mind is optimistic, you can handle stress in a constructive way. This is an ability that only those who think positively possess.

Chapter Four: Exercises to Remove Negative Self-Talk

Your reality is created by what you think and every thought you have is developed based on the beliefs you hold in your mind. When you are aware of what is happening in your mind and you take control of it, you change your innate beliefs and thoughts that are responsible for making you who you are.

The previous chapters talked about what negative self-talk are and how you can silence your inner voice. This chapter leaves you with some exercises that will help you deal with negative thoughts. You can perform these exercises when you are aware that you are thinking negatively.

You may have told yourself that you will practice these exercises regularly because you are willing to change the way you think. However, you may lead a busy schedule, and therefore, it becomes difficult for you to perform these exercises. Therefore, it is important that you set a reminder every day. Set aside some time every morning or night to perform these exercises.

Track your progress by using either sticky notes or journals. You can also use them to remind you about the activities that you must perform. Stick these notes in your bathroom, bedroom, kitchen and every other place in your house that you visit frequently, to remind you that it is time to perform the exercise. It may seem unnecessary to remind yourself in every possible way, but it is essential since you are changing the way you talk to yourself. Let us look at some exercises that you can perform regularly to change the way you think.

Ho'oponopono Process

The Ho'oponopono Process is an ancient Hawaiian healing process that works on your energy. This exercise has helped many people remove negative thoughts and foster positive thinking. When you perform this exercise, you not only alter your external reality, but also change your body. This is because the process works only on your energy and uses that energy to heal you. You should look at some of the different explanations available on the Internet to help you understand the process better. You can learn more about the process in the following article: The Updated Ho'oponopono and Dr. Joe Vitale's Zero Limits.

Affirmations

It is obvious that positive affirmations are a great way to start thinking positively. Depending on what your needs are, you can choose any positive affirmation and repeat that throughout the day. With affirmations, you can change your negative thoughts into positive thoughts. This means that you should keep your thoughts in check and immediately use a positive affirmation which will lift you up and help you change the belief that is giving you this thought. Through affirmations, you can identify the beliefs that make you think negatively. You can replace or remove those beliefs with positive affirmations and beliefs. Affirmations work since they work on the principles of the law of attraction. You attract what you believe.

Short Stories

In this method, you can tell yourself a short story that you have written which brings some happy and positive images to your mind. You can use this method when you feel low or are having a bad day. You can use this method in two ways:

- Like the previous method, when you find yourself thinking negatively about a situation, stop yourself. Instead of using affirming thoughts, you can tell yourself a story of how the future can look for you. You can also tell yourself about your hopes and dreams. When you are good at this, you will stop worrying yourself with negative thoughts and create a better space for yourself. You will learn to expect that only good things will happen.

- The second method is like the first, except for the fact that you will tell yourself a story that is not related to the negative thought. You cannot expect to always think positively because it is not something that is good for the mind. Therefore, it is best to avoid negative thoughts in any situation and replace them with a story about an unrelated topic. To do this, you should tell yourself a story of your possible future that is related to any other aspect of your life.

Good Memories

Stuart Killan

One of the most common things about life is that we are never in the same place in our lives every step of the way. There is something that constantly changes in our lives. You can deny this, but there is always a small or big change in life. You may be better at a task or things may have taken a turn for the worse.

It can be that you are not doing well in a specific area in your life, and this part of your life was better at some point. Things may not have been great then, but it never bothered you. So, all you need to do in this situation is tell yourself about an event that happened in the past where things were always right. This will help to control any negative emotion you may have about the situation.

Your friends will often remind you about the good times. Even Facebook reminds you about a memory of yours from four years ago. Cherish those memories. You do not have to become the person you were a few years ago. All you must do is realize that this moment is precious and it will be a memory in the distant future.

Regardless of how you feel, it is important to talk to yourself about some moment in your past that left an impression on you. This memory will help you change your mindset.

Conclusion

Everybody goes through a phase in life when they think negatively about how the situation is. However, if most of the thoughts that run in your mind are negative, you will only have a pessimistic outlook on your life. These negative thoughts stem from your inner beliefs. Your inner critic voices these beliefs out and tells you that you are not good at doing anything. It is important that you remove these negative thoughts to ensure that you lead a happy life.

Over the course of the book, you will gather information on what negative self-talk is and how you can identify it. You will also learn how to silence this voice and focus more on the positive aspects of life. There are some exercises in the book that will help you change your beliefs and thoughts. Practice these exercises regularly to ensure that you lead a happy life.

I wish you luck on your journey.

Manufactured by Amazon.ca
Bolton, ON

25310047R00023